1000 DOT-TO-DOT
MASTERPIECES

Thunder Bay Press
An imprint of Printers Row Publishing Group
A division of Readerlink Distribution Services, LLC
10350 Barnes Canyon Road, Suite 100, San Diego, CA 92121
www.thunderbaybooks.com

Printers Row Publishing Group is a division of
Readerlink Distribution Services, LLC.
The Thunder Bay Press name and logo are trademarks of
Readerlink Distribution Services, LLC.

All notations of errors or omissions should be addressed to Thunder
Bay Press, Editorial Department, at the above address. All other
correspondence (author inquiries, permissions) concerning the
content of this book should be addressed to The Ilex Press,
Carmelite House, 50 Victoria Embankment, London, EC4Y 0DZ

For Ilex:
Executive Publisher: Roly Allen
Commissioning Editor: Zara Larcombe
Assistant Editor: Rachel Silverlight
Senior Specialist Editor: Frank Gallaugher
Senior Project Editor: Natalia Price-Cabrera
Art Director: Julie Weir
Cover Designer: Anders Hanson
In-house Designer: Kate Haynes
Senior Production Manager: Peter Hunt

For Thunder Bay:
Publisher: Peter Norton
Publishing Team: Lori Asbury, Ana Parker, Laura Vignale, Kathryn Chipinka
Editorial Team: JoAnn Padgett, Melinda Allman, Traci Douglas
Production Team: Jonathan Lopes, Rusty von Dyl

ISBN: 978-1-62686-460-3

Printed in China

20 19 18 17 16   4 5 6 7 8

THOMAS PAVITTE

1000 DOT-TO-DOT
MASTERPIECES

THUNDER BAY
P·R·E·S·S
San Diego, California

TWENTY ICONIC WORKS OF ART TO COMPLETE YOURSELF
PLUS ONE 19" X 14" POSTER

INTRODUCTION

We all remember dot-to-dot drawings from our childhood—puzzles that kept us happy and busy for a few minutes as we tried to work out what surprises were hidden in the mysterious dot patterns.

1000 Dot-to-Dot Masterpieces revolutionizes this timeless activity, turning primitive outlines into stylish drawings with tonal shading and expressive line work. All you need is a little patience, and you will amaze yourself with what you can create with a single line. Dot-to-dots aren't just for kids anymore!

All of the dots have been color-coded to help you keep track of your position. Each drawing will take you approximately half an hour to an hour to complete, and you will be rewarded with a genuine piece of art that you can easily remove and display. It's fun for all ages trying to guess what you are drawing as you link up the dots, and it is a perfect rainy day or holiday activity.

Not only is this book a fun new way to discover art, it's also a great way of teaching kids about the principles of drawing. Through the process of joining up the dots, they will see how the lines build to create areas of tone and give the images a sense of depth—much more sophisticated than the usual one-dimensional dot-to-dot drawing.

TIPS

- Make sure the pen you use is not too thick; test it on the opposite page before you get started.

- Always start at number 1 and don't jump ahead or go backwards.

- The finished pieces look their best from a distance. Stand back to really enjoy them!

- If you make a mistake by connecting the wrong numbers, don't worry, it won't ruin the final outcome. Just carefully carry on.

ABOUT THE ARTIST

Thomas Pavitte, born in New Zealand in 1985, is a graphic designer and experimental artist who often uses simple techniques to create highly complex pieces, and whose dot-to-dot pieces have been enjoyed by people all over the world. He set an unofficial world record for the most complex dot-to-dot drawing in 2011 with his version of the Mona Lisa, in 6,239 numbered dots, which took him weeks to prepare and nine hours to complete. See more of his work on his website thomasmakesstuff.com and purchase limited edition prints at his online store.

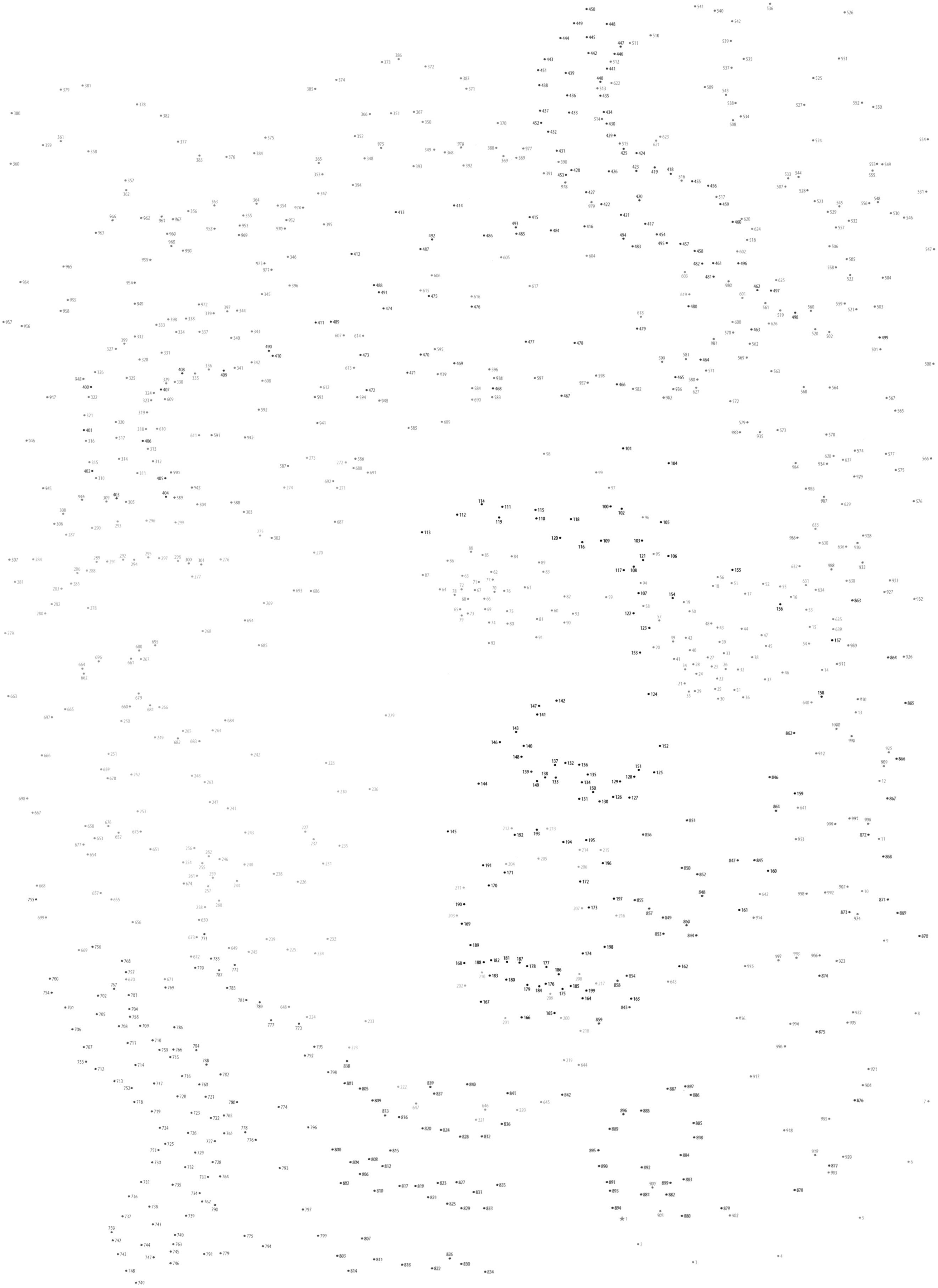

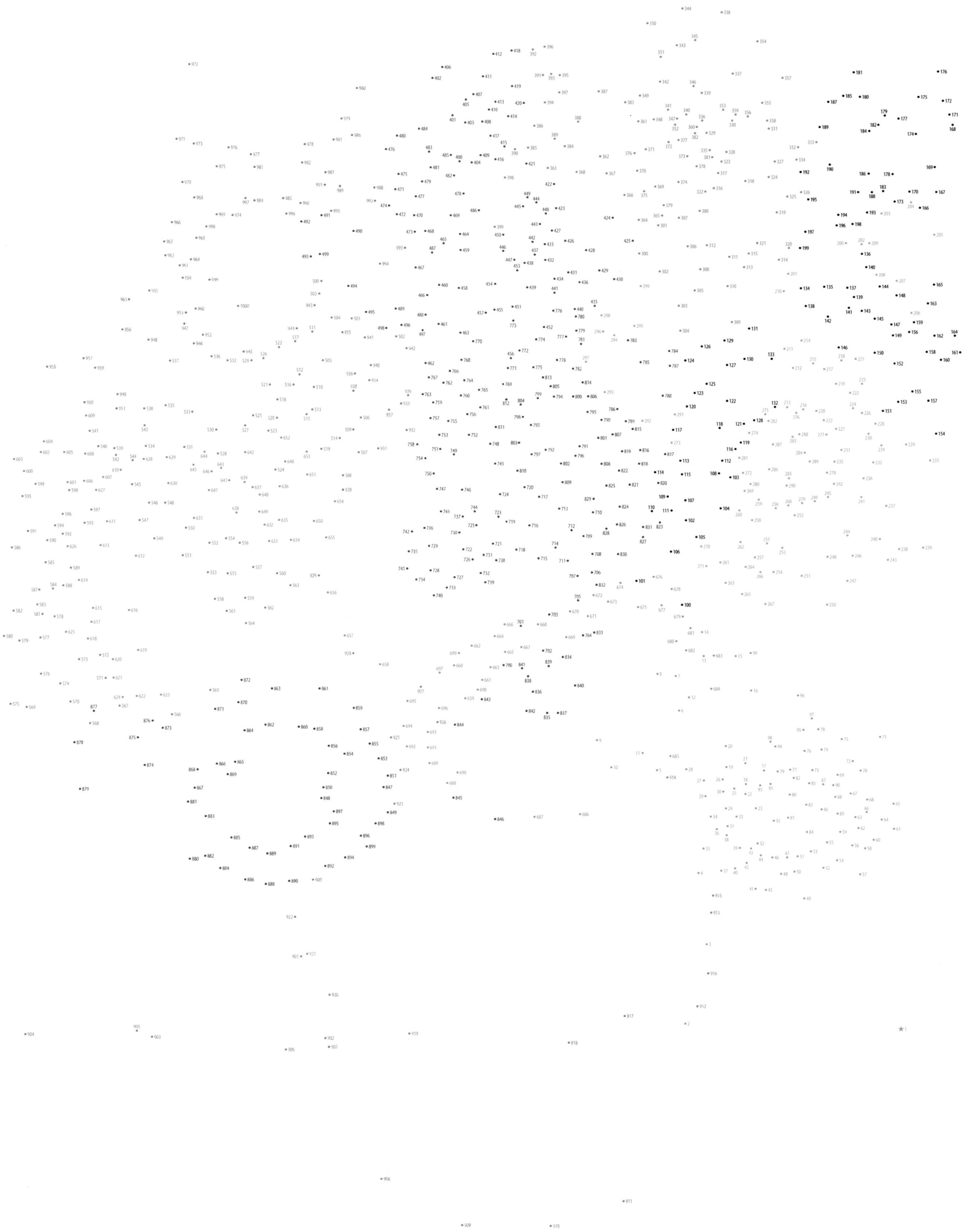

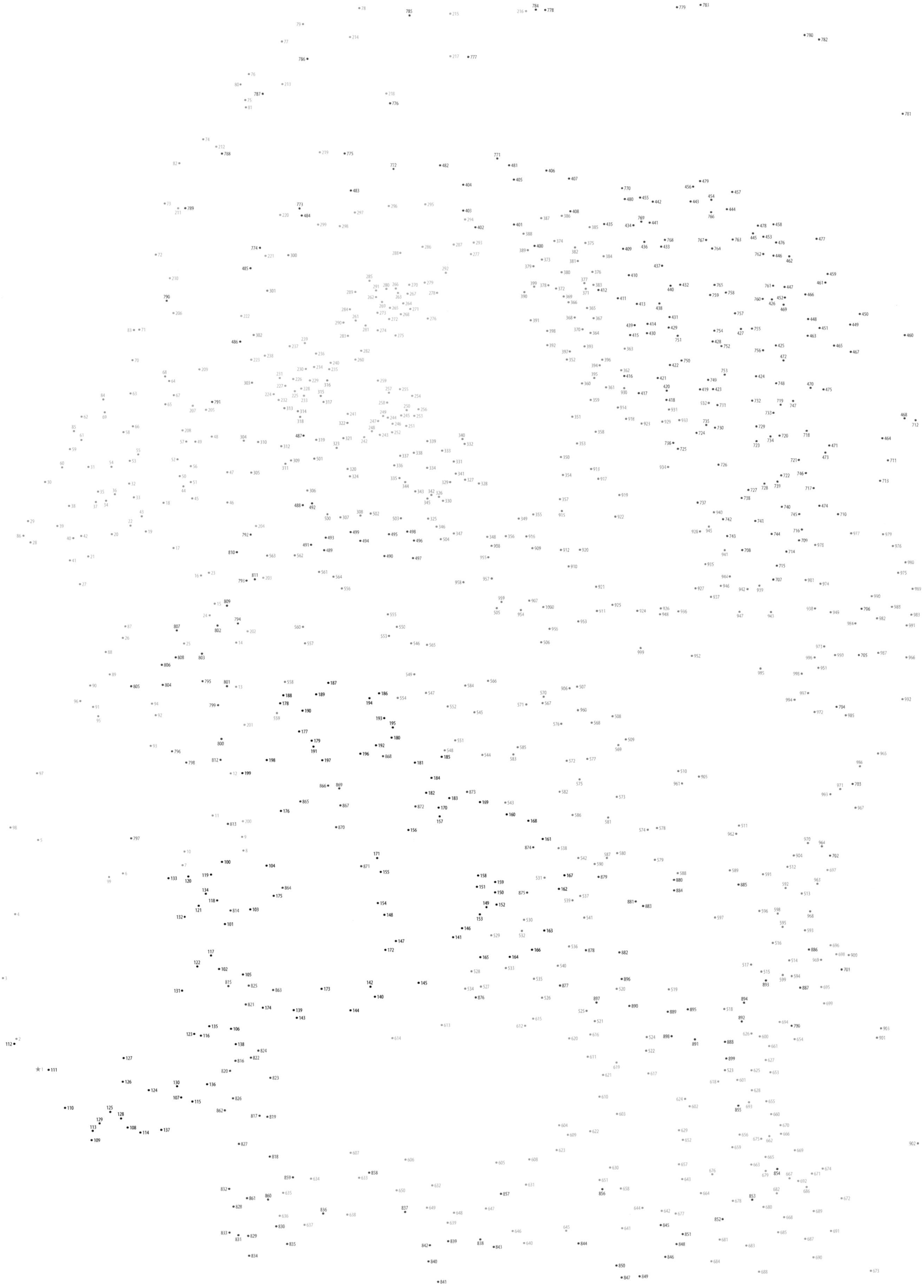

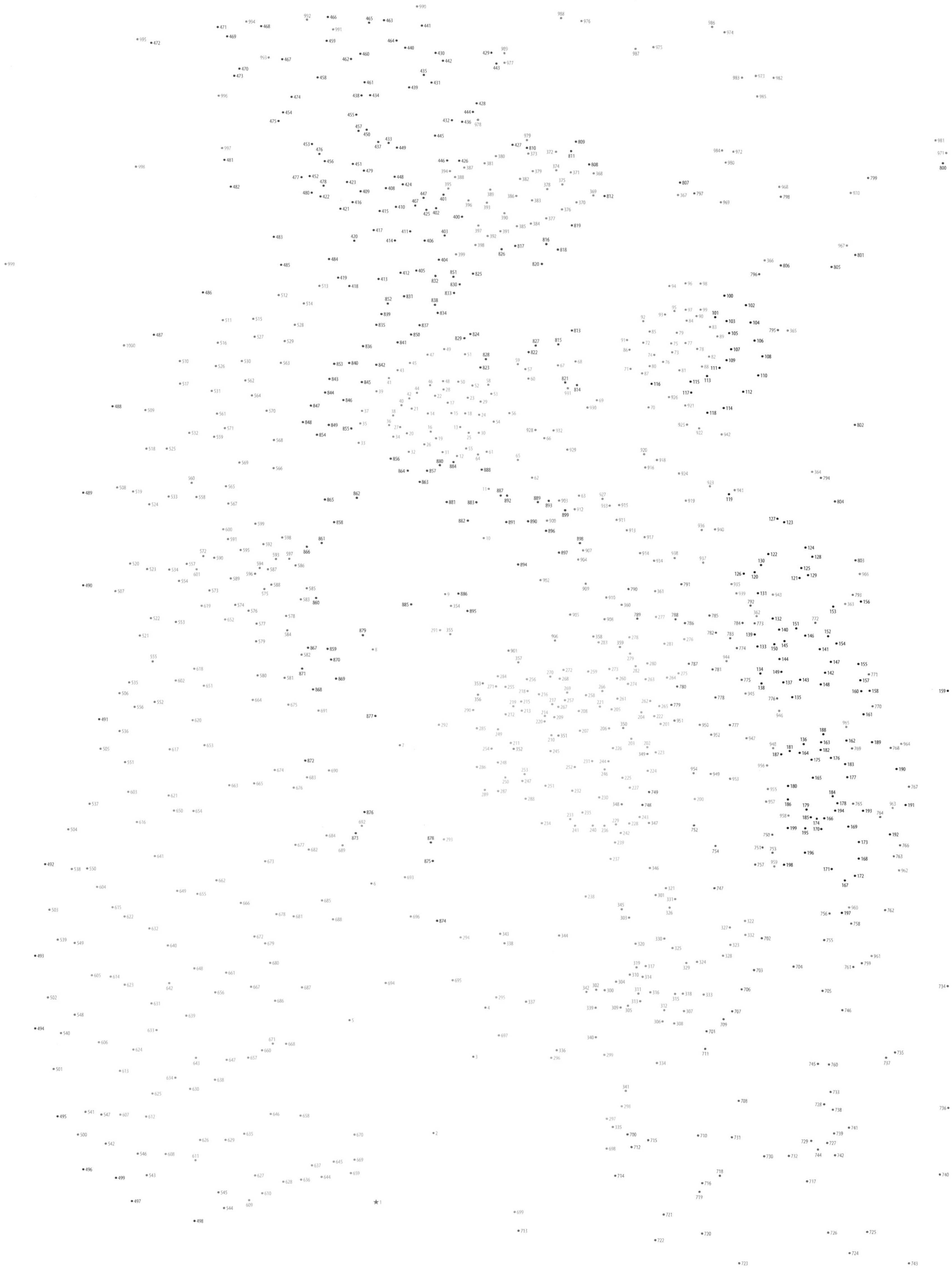

JAN VAN EYCK
Man in a Turban

PIERO DELLA FRANCESCA
Portrait of Battista Sforza

SANDRO BOTTICELLI
The Birth of Venus

MICHELANGELO BUONARROTI
David

LEONARDO DA VINCI
Self Portrait

HANS HOLBEIN THE YOUNGER
Portrait of Henry VIII

MICHELANGELO MERISI DA
CARAVAGGIO
Medusa

JOHANNES VERMEER
Girl with a Pearl Earring

JACQUES-LOUIS DAVID
The Death of Marat

WILLIAM BLAKE
Newton

KATSUSHIKA HOKUSAI
The Great Wave Off Kanagawa

JAMES ABBOT MCNEILL WHISTLER
Arrangement in Grey and Black No. 1:
"Whistler's Mother"

VINCENT VAN GOGH
Sunflowers

C. M. COOLIDGE
A Friend in Need

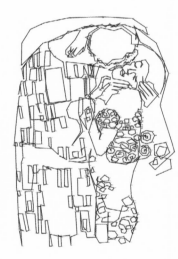

GUSTAV KLIMT
The Kiss

GRANT WOOD
American Gothic

TAMARA DE LEMPICKA
Young Lady with Gloves

PABLO PICASSO
Weeping Woman

FRIDA KAHLO
Self Portrait with Thorn Necklace
and Hummingbird

ROY LICHTENSTEIN
Whaam!

ACKNOWLEDGMENTS

· ·

Thank you to all the artists whose work features in the book, and thank you to all the artists whose works make the world a more beautiful, stimulating, and inspiring place to live in.